WHEN MY
EYES OPENED

MICHAEL SANDERSON

WWW.TRUEVINEPUBLISHING.ORG

When My Eyes Opened
Michael Sanderson

Published by
True Vine Publishing Co.
810 Dominican Dr.
Nashville, TN 37228
www.TrueVinePublishing.org

Printed in the United States of America—First printing.

CONTENTS

CHAPTER ONE

WHEN MY EYES OPENED

––––––+·+·+:+:+:+:+:+:+:+:+:+:+:◇:+:+:+:+:+:+:+:+:+:+·+·+––––––

When I opened my eyes, I knew something wasn't right. Something bad had just happened—something really bad. I was lying flat on my back in a hospital bed, staring up at the ceiling. Metal rods were inserted into both sides of my neck, holding my head in place. A rigid halo brace had been screwed so deep into my skull and upper back that the pressure left my skin raw and tender—like exposed meat.

I was bandaged up like a mummy, hooked to a massive machine that my life seemed to depend on, and pierced with enough needles to make me look like a human pincushion. I couldn't move. I couldn't speak. I was completely helpless.

Three nurses moved around me with focused urgency, working diligently to tend to my bruised and broken body. Family members sat quietly around the bed, their faces a mix of worry and gratitude. My on-again, off-again ex-girlfriend was there too—right by my side, her eyes fixed on me with overwhelming love.

I waited, desperate for someone to explain what was really going on.

I had a million questions racing through my mind, but no one offered any real answers. They were all tight-lipped, keeping the worst of it to themselves. The only thing anyone told me was that I had been in a bad accident—something about my truck.

But the only thing I truly cared about in that moment was whether I had hurt anyone else.

"No, everybody was okay," someone finally said. "Just a couple of cars got messed up, but everyone walked away."

Relief washed over me. Even though I was lying broken in a hospital bed, knowing I hadn't seriously hurt anyone else took a heavy weight off my chest.

Somehow, I felt comforted. Even though I was stretched out—barely able to move, barely able to breathe—knowing I hadn't harmed anyone else lifted a ton of bricks off my chest. Waking up just inches from death was terrifying, but there was one bright spot in the middle of all that darkness: I had woken up. That alone was a blessing.

It felt good—so good—to still be alive.

Just 28 days earlier, I'd been in a wreck so horrendous, most people wouldn't have made it out. The doctors and nurses told me that straight up. Chiropractors were shocked by the X-rays. My church family said it had to be the hand of God. Some folks even said I'd cheated death—and come out on top.

I didn't see it as winning anything. I just knew I was grateful to still be breathing.

For those 28 days I was unconscious, I remembered absolutely nothing. It was like being erased from time. And it got me thinking—when we leave this world, do we even know we're gone? Are we aware? Or is it just... silence?

As for heaven or hell, I truly believe it all comes down to how you lived your life.

That brings me to something I have to say: do you believe in spirits? I do—and I'll tell you why.

While I was asleep, not even knowing whether I was still in this world or the next, a question haunted me over and over again: If I hadn't made it through, where would I be right now?

I don't have the perfect answer. I could be wrong. But then again, who really knows? Only one Person knows for sure.

But here's what I believe: if you were a good person on this earth—church-going, praising God, doing your best to live right—I think your spirit doesn't just disappear. I believe it returns. Maybe, just maybe, it enters into a new life. Into a pregnancy. Into someone else starting fresh.

You can go to church seven days a week. You can be the kindest, most generous person in the world. But if you don't know Jesus—if you don't have a real relationship with Him—you will not make it into Heaven. It's not about religion; it's about relationship.

The Word of God makes it clear in Romans 10:9–10:

"If you confess with your mouth that Jesus is Lord and believe in your heart that God raised Him from the dead, you will be saved.

For it is by believing in your heart that you are made right with God, and it is by confessing with your mouth that you are saved."

And the Scriptures also say, "Anyone who believes in Jesus will not be disappointed."

That tells me there's only one way in—through our Lord and Savior, Jesus Christ. No shortcuts. No exceptions.

Now, as for heaven or hell—and what happens after we leave this life—I have my own thoughts. If you lived right, I believe your goodness carries on through another good soul, another pure spirit born into this world. But if you lived a hard life—chose the streets, the wrong paths, crime, destruction—I believe that spirit, that energy, continues in another life the same way.

Again, I'm not claiming to be a preacher or a prophet. I could be wrong. These are just thoughts that came to me while I was suspended between life and death. When you're that close to the edge, you start wondering about these things in a deeper way.

But one thing I'm sure of—you wouldn't remember your past life even if you did come back. When you're born again, you start fresh. New organs. New mind. New body. You wouldn't wake up as a baby saying, "I remember my old life. I used to love motorcycles and peach cobbler."

That's not how it works. You start from zero. And maybe that's God's mercy in action—giving you a clean slate.

As for me, before the accident, I was living my dream. Driving that big rig. Feeling free. Feeling fulfilled. And then, in an instant, everything changed. My life was nearly taken in a single moment. But somehow—through grace and a miracle I still don't fully understand—I survived.

Since I was a youngster, I always pictured myself behind the massive wheel of a big work truck. I'd see those eighteen-wheelers rolling down the highway and think, *That's going to be me one day.* And sure enough, when I grew into a man, I became the one in control of that steel giant.

Funny how life works. The very thing I loved—the thing I dreamed of since I was a boy—nearly took my life.

According to the police report, I ran a red light. Truth be told, I don't remember if I did or didn't. That's not like me—it's completely out of character. But I don't remember the accident at all. Nothing. Just a blank space. Still, one thing I do know: if I had hit those other cars head-on, the crash would have killed them. No question.

Everything happened too fast to process. One minute I was driving. The next, my world went black. My body was tossed around inside the truck like a lifeless ragdoll, slamming against the interior. When the tumbling finally stopped, I was upside down, my entire body weight crushing down on my head.

I wasn't wearing a seatbelt. I'll be honest about that. But here's the crazy part—the doctors said if I had been buckled in, the strap would've likely snapped my neck or strangled the life out of me. As wild as it sounds, not wearing that seatbelt might've saved my life.

When the rescuers finally cut me out of the wreckage, they had no idea what was wrong with me. I had a massive bruise in the center of my forehead. My skin was burned from the muffler, which had shot through the passenger-side window like a flaming cannonball.

By the time the ambulance got me to Huntsville Hospital, my body had ballooned to nearly twice its normal size. I was unrecognizable. It took about a week for the swelling to go down enough for doctors to really examine me.

At first, they thought it was just the impact—maybe trauma from the blow to the head. But it wasn't that simple.

What I had was far more serious. And they would soon discover that what was going on inside me was more dangerous than anyone had imagined.

The doctor on call that night was a neurosurgeon named Dr. John Johnson. And let me tell you—it was nothing short of divine intervention that he was the one there. Not every hospital visit puts you in the hands of a top-tier specialist, but God made sure that when I came in, the right person was standing by.

After checking me out, Dr. Johnson stepped out to talk to my family.

"This boy has hurt himself pretty badly," he told them, his voice serious and measured. "You may want to start thinking about funeral arrangements. Statistically, 97% of people with this kind of injury don't survive."

Then he paused, looked them in the eyes, and said, "I'm going to perform the surgery. But if he does survive, he'll be paralyzed from the neck down."

The diagnosis was chilling: internal decapitation. I had broken my neck at the C1 vertebra—the bone responsible for all major physical movement. Talking. Walking. Eating. Breathing. Without it, there is no you. And mine had snapped.

To put it plainly, my head was no longer connected to my body in the way it was supposed to be.

I'm a big guy—six feet tall and 330 pounds. And as strange as it may sound, that size saved me. My thick neck muscles were the only things keeping my head from completely separating from my spine. If I had been smaller or more slender, my head could've popped off like a cork from a champagne bottle.

The doctors couldn't determine exactly what was going on at first because I was so swollen. They didn't want to move me too much and risk further damage. So they loaded me up with medication to reduce the swelling and waited.

It took three separate MRIs before they finally discovered the full extent of my injury—my head was, for all practical purposes, detached from my body.

That night, I was rushed into surgery.

Only the grace of God carried me through that operating room. I was inches from death. My family had every reason to begin planning a funeral, but somehow... I made it.

After surgery, Dr. Johnson returned to the waiting room where my family had been sitting on pins and needles. He told them the operation had gone well. It was far from over, but I had made it through the hardest part.

Still, I didn't wake up.

I remained unconscious for 28 days. Four weeks of total darkness. I didn't know I was in this world. Didn't dream. Didn't feel. Just... nothing.

When I finally opened my eyes, I didn't recognize myself. I looked like the Tin Man from *The Wizard of Oz*. Metal covered me from head to upper back. I had been fused with titanium from C1 to C5. My head was being held on by rods that extended from my skull down through my spine.

There was also a small piece of metal attached to the back of my lower skull, locking into the rest of the hardware. Everything was connected—fused together as one solid unit. The halo brace was anchored to my head with four screws drilled directly into my skull. It wasn't just for support—it was the only thing physically keeping my head attached to my body.

It was surreal. I had become part man, part machine. But I was alive. And that meant everything.

Through those 28 days I was asleep, my family never left my side. They stayed at the hospital, prayed over me, whispered encouragement even when I couldn't hear it. Their love never wavered.

But what touched me most—what still brings tears to my eyes—was her.

My ex-girlfriend, the one I had just recently separated from, stayed too. She didn't have to. But she did. Day and night, she sat by my bed. She held my hand, talked to me like I could hear her, and made sure I was never alone.

For the entire two-and-a-half months I was bedridden, she was there.

13

She put her life on hold. Arranged for her mother to care for her children. Every morning, her mother got them ready, made sure they got to school—despite the fact that she lived 20 minutes from our place and the school was another 30 minutes in the opposite direction. It wasn't convenient. It wasn't easy. But they made it work.

And I'm forever grateful—for her sacrifice, her loyalty, and her love in the face of uncertainty.

When I was at my lowest, broken and unconscious, they stood in the gap for me. And I thank God for them every single day.

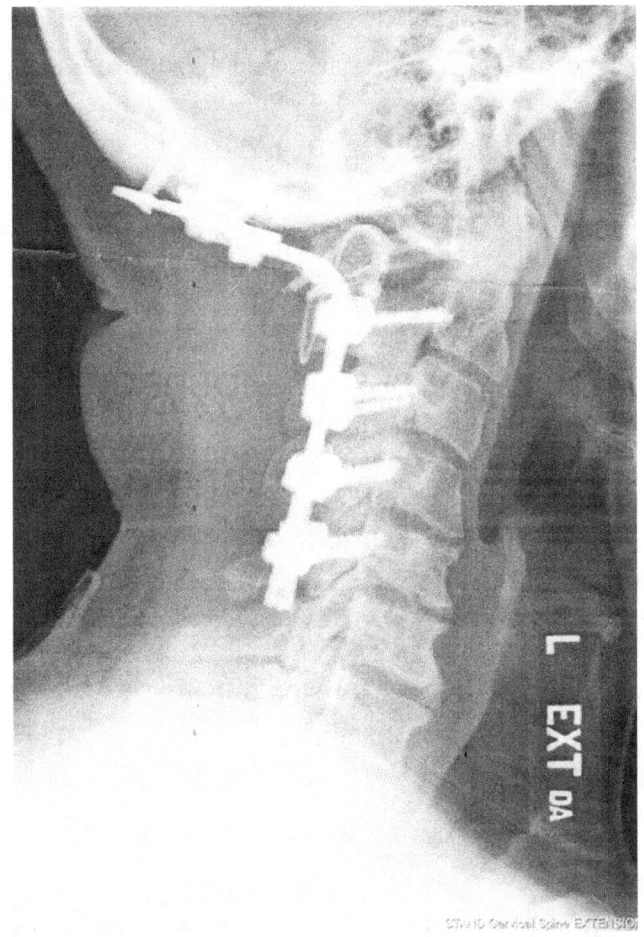

This is my x-ray, showing how my vertebrae were fused with titanium from C1 to C5 to hold my head onto my body

During those 28 days in a coma, I engaged in countless conversations with my Heavenly Father. Even though I couldn't speak out loud, my spirit was wide awake, talking to Him. I believe God was weighing it all—deciding whether I had done enough good to

15

remain here on His Earth. And while I lay there, lifeless in the natural, people all around me were sending up powerful prayers.

One of the strongest prayer warriors was my next-to-older sister, Sharon. She's a true believer—a real church-going woman of faith. She prayed over me constantly, not just asking God for healing, but going to battle in the spirit. She prayed demons out of me.

See, this kind of prayer—the laying on of hands, speaking life over the body—that's something passed down from the old generation. The elders believed that when you're near death and people of faith begin to pray over you, the Spirit of the Lord steps in and does what no medicine can do. If your body starts reacting—like twitching, coughing, or even flinching—it's believed that demons are being cast out.

That's what was happening when Sharon prayed. She would stand by my bed and call on the name of Jesus, and my body started to respond. Movements. Jerks. Shudders. At first, the doctors didn't know what to make of it.

Sharon didn't just pray—she left her mark in that room. She taped a written prayer on the wall above my bed. Every person who walked in, whether nurse, doctor, family, or friend, saw that prayer and read it aloud. It became a rhythm in the room. A covering. All day long, those words were being spoken over me.

And I believe that prayer is one of the reasons I'm still here today.

That prayer kept God's hand on me.

I can't say "thank You" enough to the Lord. Every time I think about it, all I want to do is praise. THANK YOU, GOD.

As the days passed and I stayed unconscious, my family started to notice something strange—my body began moving. Not once. Not twice. Repeatedly.

Before that, I had been completely still—lifeless. The doctors had warned my family to prepare for permanent paralysis from the neck down. They were certain I wouldn't move again.

But my body started proving them wrong while I was still asleep.

They didn't have an explanation. Movements that weren't supposed to be happening... were. Little signs that something deeper was going on. Something that didn't line up with their charts or scans. Something divine.

They were witnessing the impossible. And the only explanation? God was still writing my story.

As time rolled on and I continued lying there in that hospital bed, the doctors and my family started planning for what came next. They had to figure out a long-term care plan—specifically, what kind of physical

17

therapy I would need if and when I woke up. Eventually, they connected with a hospital in Birmingham that specialized in the type of therapy my condition required.

But there was a complication: I still had tubes in my mouth and was hooked up to all kinds of machines—breathing, feeding, monitoring everything you could imagine. Birmingham wouldn't accept me in that condition. If I was going to be transferred, they had to remove the tubes and perform a procedure called a tracheotomy. They would insert a "trach"—a small breathing tube placed directly into my windpipe—to replace the bulky equipment I was currently attached to. It was the only way I could be cleared for transport.

During all of this, while I was still in a coma, my family said I kept calling out one name: Dion.

Dion is my nephew, and he's more like a little brother than anything else. At the time, he was out playing golf with his brother Corey and their dad, Clifford. Now, here's where our family tree gets a little... interesting. Clifford is both my uncle and my brother-in-law. He's my dad's brother—so, my uncle—and he's also married to my sister. Since my sister and I have different fathers, there's no blood relation between Clifford and her. It might sound confusing, but that's how family works sometimes. Twisted branches, but strong roots.

Anyway, when they told Dion that I was calling his name—even while I was unconscious—he didn't hesitate. He dropped his golf club right there on the course, took off running, and made a beeline for the hospital.

In that moment, the game didn't matter. Family did.

He showed up within minutes, ready to ride with me to Birmingham and be there when I arrived at Trinity Hospital. He wasn't just there physically—he was present in spirit. And for reasons I can't fully explain, I didn't wake up until I made it to Birmingham.

Maybe it was the change in environment. Maybe it was the presence of someone I loved and trusted. Or maybe it was just time. But the moment I got to Trinity... everything started to shift.

And that's when my journey toward healing truly began.

CHAPTER TWO

GROWING UP

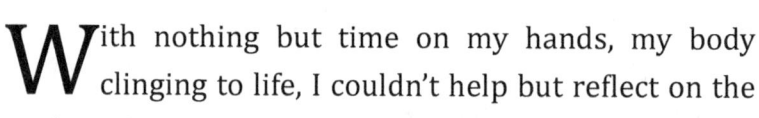

With nothing but time on my hands, my body clinging to life, I couldn't help but reflect on the trials and tribulations that these 34 years have shown me while coming of age in Huntsville, Alabama.

As far back as I can remember, my mom always took care of and provided for my siblings and me. There would have been six of us in all. Willie Jr. and Tonya died as children. I don't remember either of them because I am the baby of the family. The four of us who remained lived with Momma in Butler Terrace, one of the local housing projects in our city.

We left Butler Terrace when I was two years old and moved into a trailer park. I was too young to remember much, but that's where my biological father shot my momma in the leg with a .22. Momma knew she had to get away from that man before he killed her, so we moved into our family house on Jeri Street. We stayed there for about two months and then moved to Lincoln Projects in 1977.

I was just three years old when we moved into Lincoln Projects. I started going to the Boys' Club when I turned six. It was a local hangout spot for boys aged six to eighteen. And we loved it. We had a lot of good times there. I couldn't wait to get out of school every day. The staff there was pretty cool too. They showed us how to shoot pool, play table games, and taught us just about every sport imaginable. They helped us with our homework. And to top it all off, they even fed us. I think that may have been my favorite part.

While I was doing this on a daily basis, my sisters were busy doing other things. Two were mothers, and Nay was hanging out at the skating rink, which I would come to enjoy later. During this time, a lot of things were changing and happening. Some were good; some were bad. There used to be a corner store within walking distance of the projects called Al's Angels that we used to frequent.

There's always a corner store in the projects—even in the movies. And Lincoln Projects was no different. We would go there to get snacks or play the *Pac-Man* game. Sometimes Al would let certain people get things on credit because he knew many of the families lived from paycheck to paycheck. He was a pretty cool dude. He looked out for us, and we looked out for him as well.

Sadly, one of the guys from the hood felt a false sense of entitlement one evening and tried to rob Al. No one really knows what happened that night except the two people who were there. One of them is no longer living, so we can't ask him. The other is serving life in prison.

Despite all the temptations surrounding us—drugs, crime, delinquency, gangs—I still managed to do something productive with my young life. I got a summer job at my favorite place during my upbringing—you guessed it—the Boys' Club.

Now, I was the one teaching the younger boys the things that had been taught to me. And I was feeling good about myself. I was 15, staying out of trouble, staying in school, and working. Not only was I helping young boys, but I was also able to help Mom out at home with the extra money I was bringing in.

Mom had a job cleaning houses for the so-called rich folks who lived about 25 minutes from the projects. They paid her around $35 a day. Back then, that was pretty decent money.

Around the time I was in my early teens, most of my three sisters had moved out. It was just Momma and me now. I had no complaints, though. We did just fine and got by with a little help from one of her friends.

Meanwhile, I was busy going to school, working at the Boys' Club, and hanging out with my friends at Rainbow Skating Rink. That was the place to be on Saturday night. Everybody would be there with their cliques. Everything was cool—until somebody got the big head and thought they were tough. That's usually when the dust started flying.

There was always someone who thought they were tougher than the next guy. See, the thing about living in the projects is that you automatically had beef with the other projects—and vice versa. So if two people who had issues with each other were from different neighborhoods, war had officially been declared. Whatever cliques they were from, they'd go get their boys. Sometimes the damage was crucial.

One time, my cousin got caught up in one of those fights and was cut on his back with a razor. I guess he was so busy swinging that he didn't notice until he got back to the 'hood. It was serious enough that he had to go to the emergency room and get stitches. That boy was foolish, though. On his way home from the hospital, he saw the same guy from the skating rink—and started fighting him all over again.

Those were the days.

In the meantime, Momma was getting cozy with her new friend. They were getting real cozy. He was a pretty nice guy—and just what Momma needed. He wasn't like the usual riff-raff you'd find lurking around the projects. He had a good job, carried himself well, and lived a stable life. He dated my mom for about five years and eventually told her that she deserved better than the projects.

Now, don't get me wrong—we never felt like we were better than where we came from. It's not where you live; it's how you live. But he felt like Momma had worked too hard to settle for less, and he wanted more for her. And honestly, there's nothing wrong with that. She deserved better. She was hard-working, selfless, and had done everything she could to provide for her children.

With his help, we left the 'hood and moved into a nice house in the suburbs.

Unfortunately, by then, I was no longer in school. I had dropped out in the 12th grade because I wasn't going to have enough credits to graduate. Still, I didn't let that stop me. I kept pushing. I kept working. I kept doing what I needed to do.

And I always kept a job.

In 1996, I got hired as a janitor at Huntsville Hospital, working in environmental services. I stayed in that department for two years, and then in 1998, I transferred to the linen department. A year later, a position opened up for a truck driver in the linen department at a building in Madison.

That building was affiliated with all the local hospitals—Huntsville, Athens, Decatur, and Marshall County.

That opportunity?

That was my big break.

I had already known my true calling in life since I was a snotty-nosed little boy. And now, it was time to answer it.

Ever since I was a kid, I've always loved big trucks. I can remember standing in the street back in the projects, trying to get truck drivers to blow their horns as they drove by. I loved that powerful sound—it gave me chills. Still does, to this day.

Finally, at the age of 25, I landed a job as a truck driver for a company called Health Group of Alabama. I was responsible for delivering clean linen to hospitals in Huntsville, Athens, Decatur, and Florence.

Even though that was the name of the company, they were still affiliated with Huntsville Hospital. After two and a half years with the company, my assignment ended. I got laid off and started drawing unemployment.

During that time, I picked up a job driving dump trucks for a guy named Mr. Beacher. I stuck around for about a year, but to be honest—I got bored. Driving dump trucks was okay, but I had bigger dreams. I wanted to drive 18-wheelers.

So I did what I had to do. I figured out the steps, signed up, and went to truck driving school for two weeks to earn my CDL license.

I learned how to shift 16 gears, steer, back up, and understand all the rules of the road. If you passed all your classes, you were guaranteed a job at the end of graduation. I passed my test on the first try and landed a job with Falcon Truck Driving Company.

They paired me with a trainer, and together we hauled rolled steel on a flatbed trailer, covering the entire northern part of the country.

It was a great opportunity—but man, let me tell you... having a trainer with bad hygiene can turn that cab into a living nightmare.

Those trucks are built with two small beds—one on top, one on the bottom, kind of like bunk beds. When one person drives, the other is supposed to catch up on sleep. But it's real hard to get any rest when your driving partner has body odor that could knock you out better than a sleeping pill.

Two weeks had passed on the road, and I got a phone call from Alabama Concrete offering me a job. They offered great pay and a good benefits package. Getting paid every week, having good benefits, paid vacation, and holidays off all sounded good—but what made it sound even better was that I wasn't going to have to smell any more body odor. It didn't take a second thought before I took that job with Alabama Concrete.

I could really get used to getting up in the morning in my own bed, getting ready for work, going to work, and coming home at the end of the day. I was like a kid on Christmas Eve. I didn't know how to act. I was at home, driving a truck with only one person—me. Life was great! I had nothing to complain about.

Around this time, I was living at A224 Conley Drive in Toney, Alabama. My paternal grandmomma owned a lot of the land on that street. Her living kids still lived in that area. One evening, I got off work and made it home. I was relaxing with the family I had back then when the phone rang while I was lying in bed—it was my dad, who lived next door.

"Get up," he demanded. "I think something is wrong with your uncle."

This was his sister's husband. They lived next door to him. My aunt Irene worked 12-hour shifts, from 6 in the morning until 6 at night, at a CD factory called Cinram. My uncle was home alone.

It was not looking good.

He died in the doorway.

We got in touch with my aunt at work as quickly as we could and told her she needed to come home because something bad had happened. Boy, was it rough. Her reaction wasn't good.

Less than a week later, Uncle was peacefully laid to rest. Tons of family and friends showed up to the funeral to pay their respects. He was put away very nicely. He wore a black suit, and there was a seemingly endless array of flowers. My aunt held it together well.

Little did we know, however, that would not be the last time death would come knocking.

CHAPTER THREE

FAMILY & FRIENDS: GONE TOO SOON

My cousin Ralph Pruitt was in this motorcycle club called the Showtimers. He was a really good bike rider. He was always at my house because I used to have strippers over every now and then.

Ralph and his bike-riding buddies were over at his mama's house one night, talking and having fun. Without warning, Ralph hopped on his bike and left without saying a word to anybody. As he made it to the end of Conley Drive, he took a left turn and headed down Mt. Lebanon Road, flying at the speed of sound. All of a sudden, his bike shut off. His boys took off to see what was going on. When they made it to Ralph, it didn't look good.

They say he was going about 120 miles per hour. Somebody was backing out of a driveway, and he had to suddenly hit his brakes. He went flying up into the air, landing on his neck. My cousin was pronounced dead on the scene.

Ralph was laid to rest on May 5, 2006. People packed into Mallard Creek Primitive Baptist Church to pay their final respects. The church was so crowded that some people had to stand outside. Family and friends stood up and shared good memories they had with him. My dad got up and sang the old hymnal *"I Won't Complain."* The song was very touching for someone being put to rest. There were so many bikers there.

At the cemetery, as he was being lowered into the ground, the bikers all fired up their bikes. After all the tears had dried up and everybody went back to living their lives, the memories still weighed heavily on everybody's hearts—even to this day.

Days later, when I was back at work, I was trying to put together a song in Ralph's memory. If there was anything I loved as much as trucks, it had to be music. I loved how music moved me and made me feel. It had the ability to take me on an emotional rollercoaster within just a few minutes of sound and emotion. While I was out on the road driving trucks, music was always there.

So I felt it was only fitting that I dedicate a song to Ralph. He was my first cousin, and we were close. The song was called *"Nightshifts."* With the accident happening to him at night, that was the time the Lord was ready to call him home.

Only seven months had passed since my father delivered that moving song at his nephew's funeral when he began to get sick. He lived just next door to me.

We took him to the hospital, where he remained under a physician's watchful eye for several days. Everybody in my family would go up there, sit with him, and keep him company. One day I went up to check on him, and he was doing very well. So I left to take care of some things.

Later that evening, I got a call from his niece Emma, his sister's daughter.

"Your daddy is about to come home, and he said to go turn on the heaters for him because it's cool outside," Emma told me.

I made it home and went over to his house to turn on the heaters like I was asked. I was so happy that he was finally coming home. I got the place heated up and went back next door to my place. Time kept ticking, and I was saying to myself, "Where is Daddy? He should be home by now."

My phone rang, and it was my sister. She did not sound good.

"What's wrong?" I asked her. As I waited for a response, the seconds felt like decades.

"Daddy's dead," she told me.

"I just got a call telling me to go turn his heaters on!" I said, stunned. "What happened?"

"Emma was bringing him home from the hospital," my sister cried. "He asked her to crack his window because he was hot. She cracked the window and asked if he felt better. His head dropped down and..."

Daddy was initially hospitalized because of stage four brain cancer. He had a heart attack on his way home. It was his 61st birthday.

My daddy, George Hardin—better known as "Big Stack"—had gone home. I miss my father, but I'm glad he went in peace.

People have been telling me for a long time that death comes in threes. Even though it has happened to me and I am now a strong believer, I still had to question: does death really come in threes? Keep reading, and you will see why I made that statement.

My uncle Rose passed on April 4, 2005. Then, my first cousin Ralph died on May 5, 2006. And my daddy passed on December 5, 2006.

Everybody was put away very nicely. My daddy even had his favorite song sung over him—"I Won't Complain," performed by my sister's friend Mrs. Linda Hill. His nephew, Roy Williams Jr., sang a song that my daddy really loved as well, called "Bye and Bye." I know Daddy has no reason to complain now because he's in God's hands.

Daddy was a good man in his own way. He would cook enough dinner on Sundays for anybody who wanted a plate. That's just how much he loved cooking.

And don't let me forget about drinking and gambling. Big Stack loved his dice. He had a shed out back where it all went down. He left his family and friends with nothing but a whole lot of good memories. We think

31

about him all the time and will love and miss him for the rest of our lives.

May he rest in peace.

Through all of this death, I'm still driving my big truck every day. When I'm not driving, I'm writing songs. One night, when I was in the studio putting in some work, I got a little tired and was getting ready for bed. The news was on, but the volume was turned down, so I couldn't hear what happened.

It was another motorcycle accident, and it had claimed the life of another man in Madison—a little town not too far away. I turned the TV off and went to sleep because I had to work the next morning. When I got to work that morning, all the faces were down.

"What's going on?" I said to myself.

One of the drivers came up to me and said, "Did you hear about Dameon?"

"What about him?" I asked.

Dameon and I were close. We went to school together. He was always around my Lincoln Projects breeding grounds. He had started working for Alabama Concrete too. Dameon's truck number was 982, and mine was 983. We were crazy about our trucks. We would always turn down opportunities to get new ones just to keep ours alike.

The company we worked for had four plants: North Plant, South Plant, Madison Plant, and Hampton Cove Plant. Dameon worked out of the Madison Plant. I worked out of the North Plant. Driving for Alabama Concrete, you could easily wind up covering the entire state of Alabama.

When they told me what had happened, my heart just didn't know how to take it. Dameon was on Old Madison Pike on his bike when he collided with another vehicle. His life was taken instantly. I was down and out for a while because we had just talked a couple of days ago at his plant. And now I was burying another loved one.

After I returned to work and was finally able to maintain a clear conscience, I was sitting in my truck. The work had slowed down, and a song hit me. The rhythm was nice, bouncing around in my mind—but I had to put the words to it. It took me no time at all.

The memories of my friends and family that I'll never see again inspired a rest-in-peace song. These lives had been taken too soon. Hence the title: *"A Life Gone Too Soon."*

The song was for everybody I lost, but especially for Dameon. I have plenty of songs recorded, but the only one that's been released is my Christmas album *Love for the Holidays,* which came out in November 2004. It did okay, but not as well as I had hoped. I just had to look at where I was from—Huntsville, Alabama—a place where there's not much love for music. But just keeping it real, to all the out-of-town artists: Alabama's definitely got the sounds for you.

So here I am, dealing with all of this death surrounding me. Maybe God was trying to tell me something. Maybe I wasn't living right. Maybe I needed a change. I was wild and loose. I hosted many strip shows at my place. And before I drove trucks, I used to manage a club called The Truck Club. My stepdad, James McCartney, and his partner Willie Bradford owned the club. They'd have dancers there too—and that's where my introduction to the nightlife all started.

After a while, I got tired of that lifestyle and wanted companionship. I was married before, and that didn't work out because she loved the clubs too much. She had three kids that I was helping her raise. She didn't care about making our marriage work, and not only that, I had to deal with baby daddy drama. But I took it for the end of the road that it was and moved on.

So I'm living alone and still waiting on love to enter my life. I'm at work one day, and my ex-homeboy Mark called me up. His old lady was locked up, so he said, "You want me to get my girl to hook you up with somebody up there?"

He continued, "She meets a lot of girls up there that's looking for a man."

"Man, you think I'm into talking to somebody that's locked up? You crazy?" I asked him.

34

Then I thought about it. I said to myself, *People change,* and whoever she is, I don't even know why she's locked up. After I slept on the idea overnight, I called him the next day and said, "Okay, what have I got to lose? She'll just be a friend for now," I told him.

He told his girl, and she said she had a friend up there named Shan who wanted to hook up with me. When I found out who it was, I remembered Shan from way back in my past. I met her years prior through a mutual friend, Tony. I used to see her when I'd take Tony back and forth over to her house. Or Tony would call Shan to come pick her up every now and then. She was always looking good to me, but I never said anything to her.

This lady got my number and called. When I talked to her for the first time from jail, I told her we could be friends. I couldn't wait to be her friend. She told me a little bit about what she had going on, and I told her a little about me.

She was on work release and got out every morning to go to work. At the end of the day, she had to report back to jail. I would pick her up during the week when she got off. I couldn't take her in the morning because I had to work myself.

Sundays were like a free day for her. On Sundays, I was off, so I'd pick her up at 8 a.m., and she would have to be back by 5 p.m. The worst part of my day was taking her back to that "ruff hole," as she called it.

35

When I got her back up there, we would still have a little time to talk before she went in. Now, I'm not going to lie—I was starting to feel this woman, and I have a big heart when it comes to loving. I would hug her and give her a kiss on the jaw before she got out of the car, and I'd sit there until she got in. This woman was getting close to me, and fast. All I can say is, she knew her stuff—and knew it well. She had me, and probably still does to this day.

Months into the friendship with this lady, I wanted to turn it up a notch. Sometimes she got off work early, so I started bringing her to my place. As time moved on, my feelings moved right with it. And those were some good feelings, too.

She was young, but she knew how to handle her thing like an older woman who's got her mind right. She would cook and clean without me even asking her to. Not saying that my place was dirty and I didn't cook, but those were things she just loved to do.

Then, the loving—oh my goodness—is all I can say. Everything was all good because I had never had a woman like this. As it got close to her release date, I was so happy. What I had to get together inside of me was how I wanted to handle things once she got out for good.

Was I ready for more baby daddy drama? I got to thinking—this woman is so strong, she might not put me through what my previous girlfriends with children had done.

"It's worth a try," I said to myself.

This woman had five kids, and I was just so ready to meet them. I met them, and they seemed to be good kids. The oldest was 10, and the youngest was four. She was home free on July 12. I picked her up, and we went back to my place. My plans were not to move another woman straight in with me, but after she spent a few nights, it ended up being her home.

I wasn't tripping because she was doing everything a woman was supposed to do under a roof. After she had been there a couple of days, we ended up bringing the kids in. Now we were one big happy family—and I was loving every minute of it.

I'm still driving trucks, living good, and watching the kids enjoy their mama, because she had been away from them for almost a year. She was still able to see them whenever she was at work or got a Sunday pass, but there's nothing like being able to see, touch, and talk to a loved one whenever you feel like it.

While she was locked up, my sister put together a cruise, and when the time came to ship off, Shan would be out. She ended up paying her own way with the tips she made at work. That let me know what kind of woman I was dealing with. She was very independent— but keep in mind, I'm a pretty good man too. So if the time came that she needed anything, I was there for her.

CHAPTER FOUR

VACATIONING ON MY FIRST CRUISE

The cruise was in September, and I couldn't wait. This would be my first time flying and my first time on a cruise—and I enjoyed both of them. Everything seemed perfect. The downside was that the relationship had begun to lose its luster. I really didn't know much about her past, but I think a little of it was starting to show at this point.

Some problems were caused by me, and some by her. I know I'm not perfect and never claimed to be. But I dealt with the ins and outs for as long as I could. I was at work one day and got to thinking about what I needed to do about this situation. I came home and asked her if she wanted to stay here and rent the place while I lived next door in my daddy's house.

Shan would have to pay rent to my nephew because I had planned to remodel my dad's place anyway. Nobody had been in that house since he passed away. She said that was fine. So I went to work, buying equipment and reconstructing the place. By the time I was done, I had spent $4,500 on it. I still stayed there with her and the kids until I got done, hoping things would get better between us. I still loved her—but from a distance.

I tried my best to stay focused on my daddy's place, but it was hard being around someone you love and not knowing if it's going to work out. Sitting back and watching the kids—even though I wasn't there when she gave birth to them—I loved them so much that I felt like I was there in the delivery room. Hopefully, one day everything would be like it was when I first met her, and I hoped it would stay that way forever. She's a good girl, and she and those kids will always have my heart until the Lord sends for me.

We were out shopping and getting the stuff we needed for the cruise because the time to shove off was getting close. Now, even though this lady and I had agreed to split up and live separately, we were still living together for now. I was just hoping that on this cruise, she wasn't going to treat me like she didn't know me. From the airplane to the boat, she had me feeling like she was still all mine. I thank God for the feelings she was putting out to me—because, boy, they sure felt good.

When that magical morning arrived, we were all packed and ready to go. My sister and her husband drove us to the airport. It was still dark outside as we were on the road headed to our destination. We left that Friday morning and finally made it to the airport. As we got unloaded, my stomach began feeling kind of funny because it was getting so close to the time for us to get on this plane. Everybody was just sitting around talking, waiting on them to call for Miami, Florida. They finally did, and we all piled onboard the plane, loaded up, and were ready for takeoff.

The plane is rolling; it's rolling fast; it's rolling faster. Oh my goodness—it's lifting off the ground, and we were airborne in no time. I had my eyes closed when we started going up, but it wasn't so bad. I'm starting to like this. We had been up in the air for a while, and I looked down below. Everything was so small—but I guess it would be when you're so far up. Then they made an announcement that we were about to land in Miami.

The plane starts to ease down. I'm getting that feeling again in my belly. Things below are starting to look huge again. We are on the ground now, flying like a race car. We're slowing down, slowing down—and finally, we are here. Everything went well.

We're waiting to be picked up and taken to the hotel where we'll be staying until Saturday morning. Then we would be picked up again and taken to the cruise ship, and I couldn't wait.

When the day came for us to leave for the cruise, the van came to the hotel to pick us up—and we were ready. We got loaded up and were on the road headed to the boat. My, my, my—we're here, man. What a big boat it is.

If I'm counting right, it had nine floors. I guess you could say we were in a big building that floats on water.

We're about to head inside and give them our paperwork. They wanted to make sure that you were who you said you were before the boat took off.

So we're all ready to go up to our rooms. They had three different room types. They had the regular one, which we were in. It was okay—we just had to push both beds together to make one. It was good for single people or people who were just friends. Then they had the rooms with a window, so you could at least see the ocean as the boat cruised.

Then there were the rooms with a balcony. You could go outside and sit down while the boat cruised. They also had suites, but I couldn't tell you much about those because nobody I knew—or had been with—had ever stayed in one. But who's to say? Maybe one day we'll see.

As the ship takes off, we're unpacking so we can tour the entire boat. We were only there for seven days, but as big as that ship was, it was going to take the whole time just to explore it. That ship was full of everything—casinos, live entertainment, swimming, games—or you could just go up on the top deck and relax. It had plenty of areas to lay back and take it easy. That boat had everything you could want to do, whatever you wanted to eat.

And the best part of it all was that the food was free. Yes, I said *free!*

41

The first stop the ship made was a private island where they had food cooked for us and some games. They also had live entertainment and dancing. We stayed out there for a good while, until it was time to go back to the ship. They made sure everybody was back onboard on time so we could take off and make our next port.

The next day was a day at sea. We stayed on the boat, still having lots of fun. The next morning, those who had gone to sleep woke up in San Juan, Puerto Rico. We unloaded everyone who wanted to go ashore. People who didn't want to go ashore stayed on the boat and enjoyed themselves. As we got off, there was so much going on—little shopping outlets, food (good food too), but it wasn't free.

We had a good time. There was a lot to see. They had spots set up for drinking—plenty of ice-cold beer, because boy, it was sure hot out there. They had mixed drinks too. We had a bus driver who took us all around the island, showing us many different places. One place he showed us was a big drug dealer's house. At one time, this guy had the whole island on lockdown. I think he's finished now, though. That was a long time ago. I don't have any idea what he's doing now. They didn't say.

As the sun was setting, it was time for the driver to take us back so we could load up and set sail again. I just went back to my spot at the casino, spending money—winning some and losing some. Most of all, I was enjoying myself. We're back up in our cabin, getting some shut-eye, wondering where we'll wake up next. By the time we woke up, we were unloading again at St. Thomas, U.S. Virgin Islands.

We got on another bus. This guy's wife was a police chief. He drove us all around the island, showing us a lot of little places. We made a couple of stops, and he took us to the top of this mountain. The view was lovely. You could see everything from up there. You could even see the cruise boat—beautiful.

Everything went great on that trip, so we were back on the boat enjoying ourselves again. That night, they had something set up for those who wanted to participate. They had live entertainment lined up.

As the days rolled by, I wondered where we were going to end up next, because we only had a couple of days left to enjoy on this cruise. Then they announced that the next stop would be the last stop before porting back into the States. They drop you off where they picked you up—and I was not looking forward to that.

The final stop was at Grand Turk. Rather than tour the island, we spent the day at Jimmy Buffett's Margaritaville. What a nice place that was. If they were saving the best for last, they did a good job. This place had a live DJ, swimming, food, and lots of stuff to buy. I guess you could say we partied like it was 1999.

We had a good time. There was dancing, and the DJ had it set up where you could win drinks—because otherwise, you had to pay for them. I didn't want that day to end. But before I knew it, the fun was over, and it was time to load back up on the boat. Goodbye, Margaritaville. I hope to see you again one day. And just like that, we were headed back to where we came from.

The next day, we would be on the boat all day, just having fun. So whatever it was you hadn't done yet on this boat, you better do it—because the next time you lay your head down to sleep, it'll be your last night doing so on this ship. When you wake up, it will be time to exit—and time to return to regular life.

They had all kinds of things set up for us on our last night of the journey, and we tried to partake in every offering we could until morning. When the sun came up the next day and it was time to say goodbye, the boat was jammed with hundreds of people getting off. It was time to end the tour and get back to driving trucks, raising my kids, and making my music.

We unloaded and got back on the van headed to the airport so we could fly back to Huntsville. At the airport, we were unloading, and I wasn't even worried about the flight this time around—I was actually looking forward to it. We were in the air now, talking about getting back to work. Our vacation was over, as they announced over the speaker that we were about to land in Huntsville.

I sure wasn't ready to hear that. I wanted to stay back in that fantasy land on the water. Man, I wish that boat was here with us—but there's nowhere near enough water for a boat like that where I'm from. Oh well, there's nothing wrong with wishing.

We loaded up in the ride and headed home. If every vacation could go like this one, I would love them all. My girl and I were back home now at 224 A Conley Drive, ready to unload, get in the house, unpack—and get our kids. I couldn't wait.

CHAPTER FIVE

BACK AT WORK, HEADING INTO MY ACCIDENT

Shan is a wonderful person, but before we went on the cruise, we had split up. We still went on the cruise together because it had already been paid for. On that ship, no one could even tell that we were not a couple— and that was good. We really enjoyed ourselves. When it came time to eat, sleep, gamble, watch events, or play games, we did it together. The plan was that when we got back, she would live in our old place and I would move into my daddy's house next door.

I had already been remodeling before we left for the cruise. I guess I had spent about $4,500 so far and wasn't done spending yet. When we got back, I planned to finish. We unpacked and went to pick up our babies. Every woman I've ever dealt with has already had kids, but that was never a problem for me because I love kids. I've seen how some women want to go to the clubs and get so mad because they can't find a babysitter. But the kids didn't ask to be here—they were made.

I don't have any biological children, but the ones I'm raising now are my kids. I never had to deal with baby daddy drama in this relationship. I've had to deal with some crazy ex-boyfriends in past situations. The daddies would want to act up because a real man was there taking care of their kids. But I fault the woman as well, especially when they don't stand up for themselves. I'm so glad that's over.

But here's the thing—as far as the kids go, I love them all, and it doesn't matter if me and their mama are together or not. That love doesn't have anything to do with her. I love all of them unconditionally. They always call me "Daddy" or "stepdaddy" whenever they see me, so I must be doing something right. Even though I don't have kids of my own, that doesn't mean I don't know how to be a daddy. Plus, I have a lot of nieces and nephews, so I've been trained very well when it comes to kids. Even though this lady and I are not going to be together anymore, it wasn't because of the kids that we didn't make it as a couple—so the love still remains.

Tuesday morning, back at work, I was bragging to all my co-workers about the cruise. I told them all how they need to take a vacation like that before they leave this world—not even knowing that my almost leaving this world was right around the corner. I'm not wishing bad luck on anybody, but you just never know when the Lord will call for you.

After I got off work, I went home and started back working on my place. Dark was about to fall, so I went back to my old place, which was just next door. I would take a shower, eat, and then get in bed because I had to work in the morning.

Even though my ex-girlfriend and I were not together, you really couldn't tell—because I still did things for her.

I would talk nice to her; we still slept in the same bed, even though no sex was going on. I could still hold her at night when we got into bed.

It's Wednesday morning, September 19, 2007. It started out much like any ordinary day. I woke before the crack of dawn, crawled out of bed, and got ready for work. I brushed my teeth and washed my face like I did every morning. I put on my pants and my shirt. Then I grabbed my keys and woke old girl up. I told her I was about to leave. She even walked me to the door.

"Have a good day at work, and I'll see you when you get home," she told me as I headed out. I told her, "See you, too." That was nothing but love.

I headed into the plant about 20 minutes early to service my machine and pick up my first load of cement for the day. Little did I know, it would be my last. I was about to clock in and get in my truck. I had my hood raised, checking my fluids, making sure all my levels were right, checking my tires—making sure I didn't have a flat and none of them were low. Everything looked good. I got in line and waited on a load.

"983, go East," said the loader man over the truck radio.

I got my ticket and headed to the wash rack to check my concrete and make sure it matched what the ticket said. For instance, your ticket will have a word that says "slump," and that determines how wet or how dry the concrete is.

My ticket said "6-inch slump," meaning the concrete was kind of soupy. A 4-inch slump means it would be kind of stiff. Sometimes it might even call for fiber. If so, that would be up on the rack in some bags. I got my load together and headed out to the job. My plant is on Springfield Road, so I headed down it to Pulaski Pike. I took a left onto Pulaski Pike until I got to Winchester Road. I took a right on Winchester Road.

And this is where it all goes down—from what I've been told.

I headed out the gate, and as I'm beating down the highway, sitting high up in the clouds, I noticed a two-car fender bender up the road ahead of me. I veered to the left to avoid the accident. Because my trailer was fully loaded with more than 34,000 pounds of cement, my truck swerved so hard that the extra weight shifted the rest of the vehicle and flipped me completely over.

The truck landed on its right side. The impact of the crash packed so much force that it tore the top vertebra from the base of my skull.

I was rushed to Huntsville Hospital and stayed in a coma for 28 days. Family and friends told me that I woke up in Huntsville Hospital, but I don't remember any of that. They told me I was moving around and my eyes were open. They would tell me to squeeze their hand if I knew who was talking to me—and I did. But the only thing I can say about that is: that was God giving my family and friends some sort of relief.

Just imagine if I had lain there the entire 28 days without moving or responding in any kind of way. Some may have somehow given up hope.

I had a lot of doctors coming in and out to check on me. I was in the intensive care unit of Huntsville Hospital for three weeks before I was taken to Trinity Medical Center in Birmingham, Alabama. Trinity is a specialty hospital that provides care for those who need a level of treatment between intensive care and regular patient care. After three weeks there, I was taken to Spain Rehabilitation Center at the University of Alabama Birmingham Medical System. There, they helped me with physical therapy and learning how to eat again. When you've been fed through a feeding tube for almost a month, you have to get used to solid foods again. I did—with the help of those sweet nurses and my family.

My primary care doctor was Dr. Pitts. He was at Trinity Hospital too, but I had about six or seven different doctors over there as well. When I got to UAB Hospital, Pitts was there too—but he was the only one I had to deal with. Every time he came, he made sure I was doing well. But the one thing that kept bothering him was the cut they had made during my surgery. That was also where they had to go in and fuse me with metal.

"I don't like that," he said every day he came to see me. "I don't like that," he just kept saying.

This is what my truck looked like after the accident

My cut was looking infected to him because it wasn't healing right. The infection turned out to be a staph infection. Whenever he came by to check on me, there was pus running out of it. It was always moist. The last time it didn't look right to him, he got in touch with a neurosurgeon by the name of Dr. Pritchard.

Dr. Pritchard came to see me—and it didn't look good to him either.

*Another view of the truck taken at the accident scene

Now, I'm about to have another surgery. He's going to take out all my staples, open up my cut again, go in and clean out all the infection, and staple me back up. I sure didn't like that. While performing this surgery, Dr. Pritchard found small fragments of bone and metal, which he removed along with the staph infection.

The good thing was that he didn't have to go all the way down to the metal—but the bad thing was that my cut had to be opened up again. I pretty much had a double surgery. That was no fun at all.

My body had become so addicted to pain medicine that when they gave me medicine to put me to sleep, it didn't keep me asleep very long. I woke up just as they were finishing. That wasn't fair, because I didn't get to sleep through any of the pain—I woke up right when the pain was just getting started.

After that little surgery, I was looking at about a week to a week and a half before I could get out of the hospital and be home with my family. I sure couldn't wait for that. So in the meantime, I stayed in the hospital, still going to therapy every morning, eating right, and just waiting on my release date. It was like I was locked up in jail—but I was just in a hospital.

I was just taking it day by day. Shan was still by my side. No matter what happens in my life, I will love this woman forever. Everybody was taking turns coming up there to see me. Even though they still had to work, they managed to make the trip—and that's love. Driving an hour and fifteen minutes from Huntsville to Birmingham just to see me... I felt so special.

My eating habits had gotten a little better to where my friend and I were walking down to the cafeteria to get something to eat. I wasn't waiting on that diet stuff anymore—but it wasn't that bad, though. The therapy people were still doing their job—and a good job, I must say. They had this one lady named Mrs. Sophia; she had these mind games set up for me to see if my brain was okay—and it was. I did pretty well.

They say that when you have a major head surgery, sometimes it will mess with your brain. I really don't remember what happened in my accident because my Father upstairs put me to sleep before it happened—so I wouldn't remember or feel pain. Thank you, Lord.

My days at the hospital were about to come to a close. I would soon be home, but when I got there, a nurse still had to come out to check on me and make sure everything was going okay. They had to monitor my blood pressure and temperature for a couple more weeks.

I was still wearing the halo, and I had to keep that on until December. I got released about a week and a half before Thanksgiving. It was the best Thanksgiving Day ever. We enjoyed that day out at my mother's house. We were already staying there, so I didn't have to get up and go anywhere. I remember staying at my mother's place until I got strong enough to go home.

I can still remember waking up, taking my medicine, and setting the table to eat breakfast on Thanksgiving morning. I was so quiet.

"Son, what's wrong?" my mom asked.

My head just dropped down. "I'm just thinking about the way I am now," I said to her, tears rolling down my face. "I was just thinking that the way I am now is the way I'll be for the rest of my life."

I had pretty much no neck movement all the way around. I am fused in my neck with metal that's never coming out. Just not being able to be like I used to be was causing me to have my breaking moments.

"God does things for a reason," she said to me. Those words will be with me for the rest of my life. "There's a reason why you went through what you did. There's a reason why He kept you here."

I finally got myself together. The tearful moments stopped, but the thoughts were still riding my brain.

Thanks giving is over, and we're headed into December—the month that the halo comes off. And I'll be glad when it's off because it's really hard riding in a car. You don't want to be out in public wearing one because it draws attention. So I pretty much stayed in the house and watched TV. I didn't even feel like writing songs. That was a major shock to people because everybody who knows me knows that music and driving trucks is really all I'm about.

CHAPTER SIX

WRITING ABOUT MY ACCIDENT: MUSIC & BOOK

Before my accident, I wrote a song called "On My Way to Heaven." Ever since I've been writing—for over 13 years—all of my songs have had three verses. You might come across a song with only two verses, but if so, the chorus would be longer. That song, written before the accident, only had two verses. When I was finally able to go back into my studio, I played that song. As I listened, I started thinking about the 28 days I was asleep. I believe that's where I was—on my way to heaven. The third verse just came out of my head with no problem.

In the first two verses of the song, I'm on my way to heaven—because that's truly where I was headed. But when I got up to the gates, my Heavenly Father turned me back around because He still had work for me to do. Now that I'm back, I believe He wants me to share my story with all of the nonbelievers—those who don't believe in Him. If there was no God, then I wouldn't be here to show and tell people what I went through.

I also wrote a song about my accident titled "28 Days." This song was written to let everybody know what I went through. I titled it "28 Days" because that's when I knew I was back in this world again. Then came another song called "This Feeling." When that halo came off, the emotions I was dealing with had me feeling tired of living. So that song was written in the midst of all that.

The last song out of the four new ones I wrote is my favorite: "God's Blessings." In this song, I thank God for blessing me with a new life and for the same talent He's always given me—being a pretty good writer. And if you're reading this book right now, these are the songs that come with it: "On My Way to Heaven," "28 Days," "This Feeling," and "God's Blessings." Now, the final song that comes with my book is also one of my favorites: "I LOVE YOU MAMA." Yes, God is my Creator, but she is my creation.

I hope you enjoy what you're reading—and what you hear. Be BLESSED.

As the days passed and the countdown ended, it was time to get that halo off me. My new song "This Feeling" truly captures my emotions during that time. I was kind of worried about how it was going to feel—because they had to unscrew the four screws that were holding my head on.

The man I've been calling Daddy since I was 13 years old took me back to Birmingham to have the halo removed. The doctor who did my second surgery had one of his guys take it off. I had to sign in when I got there and wait to be called to the back.

"Michael Sanderson," the nurse announced, poking her head through the door.

"Yeah, that's me," I said.

I was so ready for this thing to come off. We headed back to one of the rooms in the office. He got his tools— like he was changing oil or installing a transmission. He had to unscrew the screws that were holding the halo in position. And I'll tell you this: it was not a good feeling.

My skin and hair had grown in and connected with the screws. As he twisted and turned, my skin snapped off. My hair was being pulled from the roots—not a good feeling! When he had twisted as far as he could, he had to pull it apart.

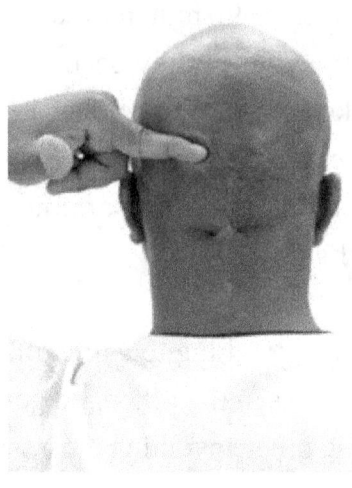

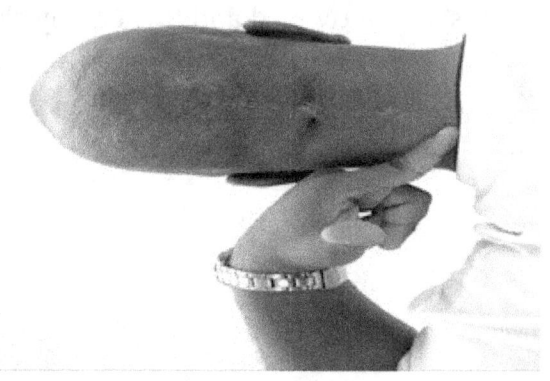

These pictures show the length of my surgery incision, from the middle of my head to the base of my neck.

"When this thing comes off," he said, wrestling with the contraption, "I'll have to give you a neck brace because the halo won't be there anymore to support your head. We'll also need to get you set up with some therapy."

The halo finally came off—and man, did it hurt. Now, instead of that circular steel apparatus doing all the work of holding my head in place, my muscles had to do their job. I may have been in pain, but it sure felt good to sit normally in a car again. Thank God.

I was still having doctor's appointments in Birmingham and would continue to until Dr. Pitts and Dr. Pritchard released me. But it felt so good to be back home without that halo. Even though Shan and the children were still at my house, I wanted to be with my mother. After everything I had gone through—and was still going through—I needed Momma around. Nothing against Shan. She's a beautiful person.

An added bonus to the halo coming off was that my favorite time of year was about to arrive. Christmas was right around the corner, and we celebrated it at my sister Doris' house—we call her Ann, as a lot of people do. We had a good time—at least I did—just being there without that halo. It was so nice.

When the holidays ended and it was time to get ready for therapy, it was also time for me to move back into my place—with my family. We thanked Momma for everything, and now I was well enough to be home. We packed everything up and made our way back to get things in order, since we hadn't lived there in almost four months.

We left Momma's house at the end of December and brought in the New Year at home. While we waited for therapy to be scheduled, the family and I just laid low. Yes, my friend and I were back together now—and it sure felt good saying that again. I just hoped it would last.

I got a call from my case manager, and he told me I'd be going to therapy three times a week at a place across from Huntsville Hospital. I called and got it set up. Everything went fine during my appointments—the only thing was, I was full of conversation. I wanted to know what exercises would help with the tightness in my neck. They told me it would help me build strength back up, because I'd lost a lot after lying in a bed for a month straight.

That went on for a couple of months. Then I had to go back to my doctor in Birmingham so he could determine whether I needed more therapy or not.

"I want to set you up for some work hardening," Dr. Pitts told me after the session was over.

"Okay," I said. "What's that?"

"Well, it's like therapy, but it's the kind that gets you back in shape for work," he revealed.

I said okay—because he's the doctor, and I felt like he knew what he was doing... I hoped. I had to get in touch with a guy named David, the therapist who was over the functional capacity evaluation test at the center where I was going. I did, and now I was back at the same place, seeing the same people—just working with him this time.

Instead of going to therapy three days a week, now it was five days a week, four hours a day—but that was cool. We walked every morning outside and exercised inside right after we were done walking. That went on for three weeks. When it was all over, I had to take a functional capacity evaluation test. That's a test that lets you know your strength level—basically to see how much you've built up since your first day.

After that was over, of course, I had to go back to Birmingham to see Dr. Pitts and hear what he had to say this time. I was with him again, and after checking me out, he said he wanted me to go back to work—four hours a day.

"Doing what?" I asked. "Do you mean doing light-duty work, like cleaning up or something like that?"

"Driving," he answered.

He wanted me to get back in those big trucks again. I was shocked that he'd send me back on the road with pretty much no neck movement. But Dr. Pitts wasn't the only doctor I was seeing—I also had to see Dr. Pritchard.

When I told Dr. Pritchard that Dr. Pitts wanted me to go back to driving, he asked, "Do you have to turn your neck left and right a lot?"

"That's the only way you can deal with a truck like that," I told him. "When you're on the job pouring out concrete, you have to watch the guys in the back of the truck—and they're moving left to right."

I'd have to climb ladders, bend over, and turn my neck constantly. With hardly any neck movement, going back to work was going to be hard for me.

Dr. Pritchard said he didn't think it would be a good idea for me to drive. I said okay. Now it was only up to my job whether or not I should return to work. When my boss found out that I couldn't drive trucks any longer, he didn't like that at all. He told me I could drive his dump truck because it didn't leave the yard.

I called my employer and spoke to Ms. Cheryl— the lady who took care of all the truck drivers' needs, including insurance, dental, 401(k), and workers' comp. When I called to ask whether or not they wanted me to come in, she was shocked too—but she said she'd get back with me and let me know something.

Some family members and I were going out of town for the weekend. We had an incredible time from Friday through Sunday. That Sunday morning, I got up and checked my voicemail—it was from the office manager at my job.

"Hey, Michael," she said. "We have some work for you to do, so be here Monday morning at 8. See you then. Bye."

"I wonder what it is," I thought to myself.

When Monday morning rolled around, I got out of bed at 6 a.m., trying to get ready for work. I usually eat breakfast in the morning before work, but that day I wasn't hungry—I was too worried about what I was going to be doing.

It's 7:30 and I'm headed to work. When I got there, everybody was so glad to see my face again. Boy, I tell you—I felt like a star. But after I found out my daily tasks, I didn't feel like a star anymore. When have you ever seen a star cleaning up for people? I went from driving a big truck to being a janitor. The one good thing about it was they didn't touch my pay. I made the same wages as when I was driving trucks.

I worked four hours a day—from 8 a.m. until noon—for a while. The only thing I didn't like was that while I was sweeping, I was stirring up a lot of dust. And sometimes the drivers would be in my way. I didn't want to ask them to move because they had work to do too. I went and talked to the boss and asked him if I could start coming in a little earlier so I could have everything done by the time the drivers got there. He said that was fine. So I did that for a while—until he decided to have me tested again to see if I could drive trucks.

When my boss found out I still couldn't drive, he didn't like that at all. He told me I could drive a particular dump truck because it didn't leave the yard. It just went to the plant next door to get gravel and sand and brought it back and forth all day. He didn't really need anyone cleaning up anymore, so it was either that dump truck—or nothing at all. Reluctantly, I took the job. But I never got to actually drive the truck because I was still being trained by another driver.

The first day I got in that truck, the boss had his son cleaning up around the plant—even though he told me he didn't need anybody for that job. He wanted to keep it in the family, I guess. But all of the bumping and banging, even for just a couple of hours, started to aggravate my injury.

While working, I was still having doctor's appointments, so I was back and forth to Birmingham visiting Dr. Pitts. On my first visit since returning to work, the first thing that came out of his mouth was, "How's the driving going?"

"I couldn't tell you, because I haven't been driving," I said.

"Why not?" he asked.

"They just don't feel like it's time to put me in a truck right now," I said.

"Okay, I tell you what. I'll find a way to get you set up for some more therapy," he said. "And I'm going to have a guy come out and do an on-the-job analysis."

David was the same guy I had been doing the work hardening therapy with. He was going to come out to my job and see exactly what I had to do—lifting, driving, and any neck movement I'd have to use. Because I was limited, he would be checking all of this out.

66

Now, two weeks of therapy were set up for me again, scheduled from 8 to 12, Monday through Friday. I had to let my job know because I'd be missing an hour and a half each day for two weeks. We got everything worked out in no time, and I was back in therapy. Dr. Pitts had scheduled me to come back one month after my last visit, once the analysis was done.

While I was still in therapy, I wanted to know what had been said in the report, so I asked David myself. I said, "David, do you think I'll be able to drive trucks again?"

"Yeah, I think you can drive again," he said.

"But will it be safe?"

"No," he said. "I think you can drive anything you want, but you're in a situation where you'd have to think about your safety first."

"Well, that's how I feel about it," I told him.

"Well, that's a decision you'll have to make," he said.

"You're right," I told him. "And I will."

Now all that was over with, and it was time to go see Dr. Pitts again. My case manager was at the appointment with me in Birmingham, just waiting on the doctor to come in. He had all the paperwork from therapy and the analysis ready to hand over. Dr. Pitts came in, got the paperwork, and looked it over. He must not have liked what he saw because he left the room for a minute. When he came back, he asked, "What kind of license do you have?"

"Class A driver's license—a CDL," I told him.

"Is that what you need to drive that truck?" he asked me.

"No, you need a Class B. But with the one I have, I can drive anything," I told him.

This doctor wanted me to go take another driving test, which would knock my Class A down to a Class B— meaning if I ever wanted to drive an 18-wheeler again, I couldn't. He told me to let my job know because if I took another driving test, it would have to be through them. I'd even have to use one of their trucks.

I made it to work the next morning and told the office manager that Dr. Pitts wanted me to take another driving test.

"Okay," said the office manager. "But first you'll need to take a DOT physical because your old card has expired."

Now, these are the doctors you go to who will only let you drive if your body is in perfect shape. She called Occupational Health Group Medical Tower and set the appointment up for me, and I went. I made it there, signed in, and they called me to the back. I explained to the doctor what had happened to me and what I had to deal with for the rest of my life.

"Son, I know you've probably already heard this before," he said, looking at me seriously. "But I'm just glad to see you here after that accident. People don't usually make it through something like that."

WHEN MY EYES OPENED

"Yes sir," I said. "I've heard it a lot."

"I don't think it would be safe for you to be out on that road in your condition," he said.

I nodded. "I agree."

"I can't give you a card," he told me. "I'm sorry."

"Okay. Thanks, doctor," I said.

"Without this card, you can't drive any commercial vehicles," he informed me.

The next day I was back at work, and I gave Miss Cheryl all my paperwork from OHG. She faxed it to Workers' Compensation. Now, Dr. Pitts had wanted to see me again after I passed this test because he planned to set up more work hardening therapy for me. The goal was to help me get stronger.

My case manager said, "Well, Dr. Pitts, if he passes this test—"

"Hey! Stop. I don't want to hear that," Dr. Pitts interrupted. "Don't say *if* he passes—just say *when* he passes this test. Okay?"

"Okay," my case manager said. "When he passes it, you want him to come back and see you, right?"

"Right," Dr. Pitts said.

Now, I really don't know how all of this is going to turn out, as far as it being a Workers' Compensation case. I had to get an attorney. I decided not to go with the first firm I had chosen. They were all family, but when I brought him my hospital bills—just from Huntsville—

he said, "This is the biggest bill we've ever had to deal with."

Just the Huntsville bill alone was $1.2 million—and that didn't even include Birmingham's medical bills. Now, the restrictions are permanent: no more driving big trucks and no lifting over 45 pounds. Right now, I'm still cleaning up for them, but they don't really need me there for that.

I went to work one morning, and Miss Cheryl told me that Workers' Comp had called and wanted to know if they had any work for me to do. She told them she would get back with them. She talked to the boss man, and he said the only thing he had was the dump truck position I mentioned earlier—the one hauling gravel and sand.

That was the only position they had open. And if I didn't take it, I pretty much wouldn't have a job. I had to talk to my attorney to let him know what was going on. He said he didn't think that was a good idea, since I was restricted from driving big trucks, but he wanted to talk to some people first and would get back with me. I said okay.

CHAPTER SEVEN

DEALING WITH ATTORNEYS FOR MY CASE

About a week had passed, and I hadn't heard anything from my attorney yet. I got to work one morning, and the office manager told me that Workers' Comp had called her and said they would be sending someone down to give me a test. This test was supposed to determine what my body would still be capable of doing.

A couple of hours later, the office manager called the Workers' Compensation people back and told them she had spoken with her boss. He told her to tell me not to worry about the test. I said okay and called my attorney to let him know they had called the test off.

"Well, that sounds like total disability to me," he said. "Just let me know if they say anything else."

My birthday was coming up, and I wanted to be off for it. I was off Saturday, Sunday, and Monday (the day my birthday fell on), as well as Tuesday. When I got back to work on Wednesday morning, the office manager came in and said, "Hey, Workers' Comp sent your attorney a letter, and we need to know if you're going to take this job. So just get back with us as quick as you can."

"Will do," I told her.

Now the pressure is starting to get heavy. I talked to my attorney again and he said, "I talked to Workers' Comp, and what they want to give you—I just don't think it's enough.

"I think when this thing is all over with, you should have at least $150,000 to $200,000. But let me talk to some people because they're just trying to get off easy."

I said okay again. But let me say this—I really didn't care about how much money they gave me, because none of that would ever equal what I've got right now: my life.

They had $45,000 on the table along with my job and the same benefits, but they would have to cut my pay. That all sounded pretty good to me, but my attorney was telling me something a bit different.

"You just do what you feel like you need to do," he said, "because they're just trying to get over."

"If I don't take it, then who's going to pay my bills?" I asked.

"You're right, and you've got to do what you've got to do," he said. "Just call me in the morning and let me know what you decide."

People always assumed what I was going to get, but whatever I receive will be because of my Heavenly Father. I was running out of time. Everybody wanted to know my decision because if I showed back up in the morning, it would be to take that job.

I was thinking real hard—but at the same time, I wasn't letting it get me down. I went to work. It felt funny being there at 7:30 instead of 5:00, but when I arrived, the boss said he'd be with me shortly. When he came back, he had their dump truck driver show me what I'd be doing.

"I've got two questions for you," I told the boss. "I need to get off at 10:30 because I have an appointment. And could I still be off every Saturday like I was before?"

"I don't know about that," he said. "Because that would leave this guy here by himself."

I said okay, because he was the boss. I got in that truck, and it felt kind of funny since I wasn't supposed to be driving. The driver showed me what to do. All that bouncing around didn't feel good to me. I was glad I was only going to be there for a couple of hours.

Before I left, I told the office manager that all that bouncing around didn't feel good for my neck.

"You probably just have to get used to it," she said.

I left at 10:30, and I guess around noon, I called her and told her I was aching really badly and was about to take a muscle relaxer and lie down.

"Okay," she said. "Call me and let me know how you're doing."

I had an appointment at the spine center to see if they could help relieve some of the tension in my neck. When I got there, I brought my X-rays from Birmingham so the doctor could see what was going on. I filled out all the paperwork and waited to be called to the back.

"Michael Sanderson," a voice called out.

I got up, went to the back, and the nurse checked me out and looked over my X-rays.

"It's just a blessing that you're still here," she said.

"I've heard that a lot," I replied.

"The doctor will be with you shortly," she told me.

What led me down here was a television commercial I kept seeing. So I decided to check them out. I'm here now, just waiting on the doctor. When he arrived, he shook my hand and told me his name. I told him mine.

"I saw your X-rays, and I just want to say I'm glad to see you're still here today," he said. "After all of this, and with what you've got going on, we wouldn't be able to do anything for you because of the way you are fused from your skull down to your C5 bone. We would hate to mess with that."

I left the doctor's office still aching from riding in that truck. I went home, put some heat on my neck, took a couple of pain pills, and relaxed. The next morning, around 2 a.m., I woke up and took another pill because I was still hurting. I didn't wake up on time, so my friend Shan called in to work for me.

When I finally woke up, I called in and told Miss Cheryl that I was aching too badly to come to work and that I might be in the next morning if I felt better. I laid around all day and got myself feeling a little better. I went in the next morning because I felt just well enough. I was back in the truck again, still not driving though.

I bounced around in that dump truck for a couple of hours and needed to see a doctor. Miss Cheryl said, "If you want to see a doctor, you'll have to go see Dr. Pitts." That's my care doctor in Birmingham. I said okay. She called Workmen's Comp and got it set up.

I got an appointment to see my neurosurgeon on April 7, which was the following week, and Dr. Pitts on April 21. I'm trying to get in touch with my attorney now because I showed back up at work, clocked in, and talked to the boss man.

"Hey, driving the dump truck is all I have for you to do," he said.

"Well, I have restrictions against driving, so let me get back with you," I told him.

"Okay, let the office manager know," he said, "and then get back with me."

That was on Wednesday. She said she would call Workmen's Comp and let them know, so I told her to call me and let me know something. She said she would call me—but she never did.

It's Thursday, and I'm back at work again because I don't want them to say that I just quit. A quitter is one thing that I am not. I showed back up again, and the same thing was said to me.

"If you can't drive a truck anymore," he told me, "then we don't have anything for you to do."

So I just waited on my check. My sister and her husband had told me some things to ask my boss Chris, but my mind was too heavy at the time. I called her, and the first thing she said was, "Did you ask him what we told you to?"

"No," I said. "I wasn't thinking and just forgot."

"I'll be leaving my house in 15 minutes, and I'll meet you up there," she said.

She showed up and started asking Chris and Cheryl questions a mile a minute. The office manager was doing all the answering, but what got to me was that she was smiling so hard—like this was all a big joke or something. I'm a changed man since I almost lost my life, so me and my sister left and went outside.

"You need to call your attorney and let him know what's going on," she said.

"I've been trying to call him, leaving him messages, and haven't gotten a call back yet—and it's been three days now," I said.

"Keep trying," she suggested. "And when you get him, call me on three-way."

I said okay. That was Thursday, and I called him all that day as well as Friday, with the same result. I left messages and still got nothing. I knew right then that I needed to find a new workers' comp attorney. But on Monday, I planned to try him again. What I was really hoping for was a workers' comp attorney—I'd heard of one who specializes in criminal cases, but I need someone focused on work-related injuries. Still, I would try my old attorney again on Monday because he really needs to know what's going on.

I didn't feel like my job was treating me fairly. I had been with this company for seven years. And even though I can't drive the concrete mixer like they wanted me to, I can't help that. Even though I didn't need a CDL for the driving job they offered me, they were still treating me like I was a stranger.

I was making $16.75 an hour, and now they wanted to drop me down to $10.50 an hour. As long as I've been there, they could've done much better than that. I'm going to try to reach my attorney again on Monday and just go from there.

Monday is here, and my sister and I talked to my attorney. He felt the same way we did—I should be getting paid while I'm waiting the three weeks to go see Dr. Pitts. He also got a test set up for me in Decatur called a vocational evaluation test, which is for workers' compensation injuries. He wanted to wait until after my doctor's appointments on April 21 and April 24.

I went and took the test he had set up for me. It was all scheduled to be done in the same week, and I was so glad. My attorney would then determine what to do from there. At my appointment with Dr. Pitts, I let him know what was going on.

"My job wants me to drive a dump truck," I told him. "I don't need a license to drive it because it doesn't leave the yard, and my cleaning job has come to an end. They don't need anybody there cleaning—just truck drivers. I never got to drive the truck, but just riding in it for a couple of hours each day was aggravating my injury."

He wrote out two prescriptions—one for the pain and one for a muscle relaxer. Then he wrote me a note to return to work with the same restrictions. I checked out and left.

The next morning, I took my return-to-work note to my boss and handed him the doctor's excuse. He wouldn't take it.

"What is that?" he asked.

"My return-to-work note from my doctor," I said.

"We thought you quit," he told me.

"Chris, I've been with this company for seven years. Why would I quit?"

He said, "Well, Workmen's Comp said anything else your doctor gives you, you need to give it to your attorney."

I left and went to the unemployment office and filed for unemployment. I took care of that, and now I'm getting ready to go see Mrs. Bramlett today, Friday, April 24, at 1:30 p.m. for a vocational evaluation test. That's a test given to all workers' compensation injuries. The test was given in Decatur, Alabama.

I'm here now with Mrs. Bramlett, and she has everything—my paperwork, my X-rays.

The test lasted about three hours, but it was all worth it.

"I know you've heard this a lot," she said. "But I'm just glad to see you here."

She was blown away by my X-rays and how I had all that metal from my skull all the way down to the C5 bone. I kind of felt like I was back in school with all the testing.

Before I walked out, she told me that once she received all of my doctors' records, she would determine a disability percentage—50 percent, 75 percent, 90 percent. She would be the one to make that decision.

Back at home, I'm chilling and trying to stay focused. I can't do any work right now. I filed for unemployment, but because my last job lied and said I voluntarily quit, they turned me down. Sitting here with no money coming in after working since I was about 14 years old—and all the way up to my accident at age 34—is not a good feeling at all. I'm a man who has worked most of his life. I've always been willing to work, and now I'm almost losing my life from working. That's tough.

But I know the Lord didn't keep me here for nothing. I still have work to do. My job on this Earth is nowhere near being finished. So, in the meantime, I'm just taking it easy until I find out what's going to happen with my situation.

CHAPTER EIGHT

MY DISABILITY & ENDING FRIENDSHIPS

—————— ++·+·═════════════◇═════════════·+·+ ——————

It's now July 2, 2009. I'm still waiting for something to happen with my case. I spoke with Mrs. Bramlett again, and she's still waiting on more of my records. It seems like Birmingham Hospital is the only one she's waiting on. Once they send the necessary paperwork, she'll be able to make her determination on my situation.

I applied for disability and was turned down the first time. I applied again and am now just waiting to hear back from them. I can't find work because of my restrictions, but I've still been looking. Not working, for me, is not good.

So now I'm just sitting here, still waiting on a verdict about whether I'll ever be able to work again. And all of this idle time at home has made me very unhappy. I'm still here with the same lady who was with me throughout my accident and recovery.

My family was going to be there regardless. But I'm starting to feel like she thinks I owe her something for being there. I do thank her for all the time she spent—because she always brings it up whenever we argue. But just being real about the situation, if I were in her shoes and had five kids, and the same thing happened to someone I was close to, I wouldn't have put my kids off on my family or friends. Family and friends weren't there when the children were conceived.

Now, I do love this woman, but something is going on inside her—and the sad thing is, she knows what it is and doesn't care about fixing it.

People used to tell me about stress, and I used to wonder what it felt like. Well, I don't have to wonder anymore because me and stress are like best friends now—and I'm not happy about it. I want it out of my life. Stress can kill you if you let it.

I never thought that a woman with five kids would bring this on. I loved the children like a biological father loves his own. But as I started to get a little better, I just couldn't take any more stress from this woman. So I told her we just needed to be friends. She said that was fine, as long as she was still under my roof. I said cool.

So now we're pretty much like roommates—and honestly, I love it this way, even though we still have our moments. I'm a single guy now, getting ready to enjoy the rest of my life in peace. My friend and the kids will be moving out at the end of the month, and I'm really looking forward to that.

She will be in her own place, and I will still be here in mine. She told me that I could still see the children whenever I wanted to, and I planned to do just that because they were really good kids—and it's not their fault that we're not going to stay a couple.

My momma told me a long time ago, "Son, you are a good man. Stop rushing into these relationships. Just let the Lord send you a good woman."

After hearing that over and over again from Momma, I said, "You are so right. I'm just going to chill and stay focused on what I've got going on. It's a new day. Thank God for waking me."

My homeboy Carl and I had some plans for later that night. He's like a big brother to me, but he had some things going on. He had an old lady at home that I'm so crazy about because she's always been like a sister to me. And even though she's not too happy with me now, I will always love her like a sister.

Mrs. Keshia, if you decide to read this book, I just want you to know from the bottom of my heart—I am SORRY.

Now back to my story. Carl also had a baby on the side that she knew about. I already knew his live-in girlfriend because we all grew up in Lincoln Projects. After my accident, he started coming to see me, and then months later, he had a bad stroke.

Shan and I stuck with him throughout his stay at Huntsville Hospital. Later, they sent him to Lawrenceburg,

Tennessee, to another hospital that offered therapy. When he got better and got out, we started having fun again. We started bowling, fishing, and going out to eat almost every day. We were spending crazy money. Even though we had five kids at home, we could afford it.

He was waiting on his disability to kick in. Whenever it did, he wouldn't owe me anything. To me, it's always the thought that counts. Once his money started coming in, our time was cut short. He started hanging around friends who weren't even there for him—but it was cool. I just stayed to myself, focusing on my book and my music.

During the time that we did hang out, I got a chance to meet his new baby's mama, Tina, and she seemed pretty cool. Now, his new baby's mama and the woman he was living with had a falling out about something. I was the one taking him to spend time with his baby. But he had to visit undercover because if the woman he was staying with found out, their relationship would have come to an abrupt end.

His baby's mama, Tina, and I stayed cool even when I chose not to be around him because the old him was slowly beginning to rear its head. I really didn't like Carl's other side. Tina said Carl always asked about me, so I decided to pop up one day, and we started hanging out again.

One of his baby's mama's friends, Ree Ree, went to Calhoun College. She called and asked me if we wanted to go out to eat at Ruby Tuesday's. I asked him, and he said yeah. We met them in the parking lot of a local motel, and I drove. We left around eight and came back about 9:30. We had all loaded back up in my van—Tina, the baby, Ree Ree, and me—heading back to the motel where their ride was.

To our surprise, Shan and Keshia were waiting there for us.

They were outside fussing, cussing, and crying. I understood Keshia being upset, but not Shan. We weren't together, even though we still lived together. We hadn't been a couple in three months. I really didn't know why she was so upset—calling my momma, telling her—as if I was going to get in trouble. Please. My momma and I are real close, and I don't keep anything from her.

Somebody had brought them to the motel in the car that Carl's girlfriend was driving, and they left when we pulled up.

Now they had to ride back with me and him. The two girls and the baby got out, and the other two got in. Riding down the street, they're still arguing back and forth. He couldn't say much because the stroke had taken his voice. The funny thing was, the only words he could say were the bad ones.

He turned around and acted like he was going to hit her, and Shan started acting crazy—opening the van door while I was driving—trying to get him to get out of the van and, I guess, fight her or whatever.

I was on the phone with my momma at the time, and she told me I needed to be careful being around all that clowning. I dropped his girl, Keshia, off at her car and took him home. Then Shan and I headed to my place. We made it in the house, and she asked, "Do you have a problem with me?"

"Yes," I answered. "You haven't changed at all. You're still acting like you used to, and I don't like it."

This was at 11 o'clock at night, and she woke the kids up. Full of anger, she told them to pack their stuff. And after everybody was packed and loaded up, she had me take them to a shelter for the homeless.

They were far from homeless, but she wanted to go—by choice. I took them like she asked and dropped them off.

The next day, she called and asked me to bring some stuff—clothes and food—to her friend's house. I told her to make sure somebody was there; she said there was. As I pulled up to the friend's house, Shan came out the door, got the stuff, took it inside, and didn't say a word. Neither did I.

I left and went on about my way. She called me again the following day and said, "I need you to come pick me up from my friend's house and take me to your house. I need to get some stuff."

Still playing her game, I picked her up, and two of the girls wanted to come, too. We made it there, and she started loading up her things. I sat in my studio until they were ready to leave. When they were all loaded up and said they were ready, I took them back, and they unloaded the van.

I left and went back home. I walked in and checked everything out, and man, I tell you—I don't know why they didn't just load up the whole house and put it in the van. They took all the food in the house, even took all the tissue—including the roll that had already been used.

I'm not mad; whatever she needed to leave, that was cool with me—just as long as she was gone.

I'm at home now, with no more stress. Maybe this stiffness that I've been feeling will ease away. I sure hope so.

CHAPTER NINE

MY NEW ATTORNEYS & CLOSING CASE

It's July 14, 2009. I'm thanking God for laying me down and waking me up this morning. I'm getting used to being at home alone again. It's nothing I wasn't already used to. I'm going to keep it like this until I get married. I refuse to live with another woman unless we are married. Until then, it's all about patience. I've just about got my place back in order.

I'm at home with no food in the house. I talked to an old friend, and she stocked me back up with groceries. Boy, ain't God good? Shan and those little babies will always be in my life because it's not their fault what's going on. I'm getting up and going for my walk like I do every morning—except on Sundays; that's the Lord's day. Sunday is for church and resting up for a new week.

I'm still waiting for these cases to be done and over. I'm still waiting to hear from my workers' compensation case, my unemployment appeal, and my disability case.

They've been gone now for almost two weeks. This will just be something I'll have to get used to. But with me being a blessed young man, I'll get over it. What I was hoping is that we could still be friends through all of this. She's making it real hard by staying stuck in the past.

She texted me one day and asked if she and the babies could use the van. I told her yes, but I had a lot to do that week, trying to make some money. We talked on Monday, and she said she needed the van on Wednesday. I asked her if she knew how long she would need it.

She said, "No, I don't, but when I'm done, I will drop it back off wherever I pick it up from."

"It will be over at my mother's house around 7 a.m. Wednesday morning," I told her.

"Okay," she said.

In the meantime, a friend asked me to do some work for her. Knowing that I had no money coming in, my family and friends looked out for me as much as they could, and I thank them so much for that. I sent a text to Shan and asked her to call me. My phone finally rang after three hours, and it was her.

"Are you sure you don't know how long you'll be?" I asked her. "Because I need to make this money so I can pay my bills."

"Well, I don't want to inconvenience you, so don't worry about it. I'll be fine," she said.

"Okay," I said.

Not long after that, she sent me a long text saying:

"I thought you were going to have something to do. Anyway, thanks for trying. If there was any doubt in my mind that I made the wrong decision about leaving, you cleared it up—because I was missing you, and so were the kids. At this point, I see that it ain't anything and never was to you. That's my fault though, for trying to give my all and hoping someone would give the same."

She went on to say, "From this point on, we do not need to have any more contact with each other," and she told me, "It's bad we are in this situation. All you have to worry about is bills."

I don't feel bad about this because I didn't tell anyone to leave. She left by choice. This was her third time leaving me and coming back. This time, I left it in God's hands. I'd like to believe that everything happens for a reason. With the serious accident I had, it was just too much weight and stress. Something had to change—and it did.

Even though she didn't like the situation, it was for the best. Thank God, because now we can both move on with our lives and enjoy peace. Time is moving on, and I'm dealing with my first cousin Emma, who is in the hospital fighting cancer.

I went to visit her one day. She had undergone a mild procedure where they implanted a tube into her, like an IV, so they could administer medicine. I stayed about an hour and a half, then went home because I had to be up early the next morning. I got up and went to handle my business and, in the midst of it all, my phone rang. I was told that my cousin Emma had anywhere from two days to two weeks to live. I wasn't expecting news like that, but in real life, it's known to happen.

That evening, I went up there to see her and man, it didn't look good. I grabbed her hand and tried to talk to her, but with that oxygen mask on, she couldn't really say anything. I looked in her eyes, and they were rolling back in her head. It didn't look good at all. Her blood pressure was so low—58 over 34, I believe. I didn't stay long because I couldn't keep looking at her like that.

On July 28, my little great-niece and I were watching TV. I called my sister Doris because my great-niece had spent the night with her, and I wanted to let her know that I had spoken with my attorney. I wanted to share what was said. I asked her how Emma was doing, and she said that since last night, she had gone downhill even more.

I finished talking to her and started back watching TV with my great-niece. Less than an hour later, my phone rang again. It was my sister. Now, for her to be calling me back that quickly, I already knew what it was. I answered and just heard her talking—I knew it wasn't good.

On July 28, around 10:30 a.m., Emma left us. We loved Emma, but God loved her most. Remember what I said earlier? Now do you believe that death comes in threes? Well, if so, how did it end up being a total of four for me? I'll tell you why: it's because death doesn't have a number, and if God is ready for you, you're leaving. It doesn't matter if it's three, four, or four hundred—when it's your time, you're going.

It's been one week now since we buried my dear cousin Emma, and the family seems to be doing okay. But this is something that we all will have to face one day. It might not be cancer—it could be something worse than that or something accidental, like my situation. Only the Lord knows.

In the meanwhile, I'm still here dealing with the pressures of my life. I got a call from my attorney a couple of days ago, and he told me that workmen's comp had an offer on the table. He wanted to know whether or not I would accept it. He told me to call him on Monday and let him know.

I hadn't been working, and all my bills had piled up on me. I wanted to go ahead and take it, but at the same time, I wanted to make sure it was what I deserved for what I went through. For the rest of my life, it will be a health situation, on and off, that I'll have to deal with.

My sister Doris and I had a meeting on Thursday, August 13, 2009, to talk with another attorney about my disability. They also handled workmen's comp cases. So we decided to put everything on the table Thursday morning at 10 a.m. The day of the meeting came, and everything went well with the new attorney.

She asked my sister if she was an attorney because she spoke like one. As we went over all of the paperwork, my sister had everything I had—even my X-rays. This is the firm I'll be dealing with from now on: SINIARD, TIMBERLAKE & LEAGUE, P.C. My old attorney is now history.

My new attorneys do everything. They even got my disability claim rolling. I have a telephone interview with the Social Security Administration on August 18 at 10 a.m. Now here's something strange to me—I would call my old attorney, leave him messages, and days—sometimes weeks—would pass. Then, out of the blue, I would call one day, and he would be there.

Now, since the small settlement offer has come up, my old attorney is calling me. But I'm not going to take that offer—and I never even got to tell him that. Ever since they received my letter from the new attorneys, he's been trying to reach me. He left me a voicemail saying the boss wanted him to talk to me. I didn't know what he wanted, and I had even called and left him a message to call me back, but maybe they were just too busy to handle a case like mine. Thanks anyway.

I needed to ask my new attorney a question today, so I called, but she wasn't in. They transferred me to her voicemail, and I left her a message to call me. It was about 9 a.m., so I went on with my day and ended up at my mom's house. Around 7 p.m., I was sitting there talking to my sister on my mom's house phone when my cell phone rang—it was my attorney. I thought she'd wait and call the next day since it was a little late, but she told me she had been tied up all day and was just now getting a chance to return my call.

I thanked her and told her I just wanted to ask a couple of questions. We talked for a little while, and she told me I had three cases going on with them. I didn't know that. I thought it was just two. But besides the workers' comp and disability case, I also had a third case called a third-party disability case. That's where the concrete truck I was driving comes into play, making it a third-party liability case.

We also had a phone interview today with Mrs. Brown, who's a part of the new law firm. It went pretty well—lasted about an hour and a half—but it was worth it. They had plenty of questions about the accident: all the doctors I saw, all the medications, the therapy, the hospitals—everything related to my injury. My disability appeal is moving forward. Thank God.

On Tuesday, August 25, 2009, we had a meeting with another attorney to talk about the third-party case involving the concrete truck. We talked for about 30 minutes, and he told me he was going to get on the case right away because if there was one, it would need to be filed before September 19, 2009. The reason is that would mark two years since my accident, and after that, the case would be worth nothing. He told me to make an appointment to come back one week before that two-year mark.

I'll never forget what he told me before I left: "I've been doing attorney work like this for 30 years," he said, "and I've never had a case as bad as yours. We've had some serious neck injuries—some that even left people paralyzed—but your injury was worse than theirs. And you're still up, walking, and pushing through all of this."

His last words before we departed were, "It is very good to be working with a miracle man."

He shook my hand and said, "Take care, miracle man."

Monday morning, August 31, I was about to call my attorney's office and set my appointment. I also planned to talk to them about some financial help. All my bills had piled up on me, and I needed some support. I was hoping they could help because here's the thing: if they could give me the money, they knew they would get it back—since when I get my settlement, the money goes to my attorney first.

Tuesday, September 9, I wanted to talk to my attorney about another possible lawsuit. I wasn't sure, but I brought it up. I told her something I had forgotten to mention before: I had to have a second surgery because when Huntsville Hospital performed the first one, they left broken bones and metal in my incision when they stapled me up.

When they sent me to Birmingham, the doctor there saw that it had developed an infection, which led to another surgery. She said they could try, but it would be difficult because things like that can happen. So I told her what my sister Doris—my second mama—told me. She said they did take care of me and saved my life, so she wouldn't worry about another lawsuit.

"But Sis," I defended my thoughts, "I've got to say something on that. God saved my life—the doctor was just the vessel He used to do it."

After I was just about done talking to my attorney, I asked her about setting up an appointment with another attorney.

"Okay," she said. "Hold on for a minute."

She came back to the phone and said she had just talked to the attorney. He told her to let me know that, as far as that third case, it wasn't going to go forward because the police report said the accident was my fault.

"I know you don't remember," she said.

"No, I don't," I told her. "But hey, we still have two cases that are pretty much a go."

"You're right," she said.

We told each other have a good day and departed.

CHAPTER TEN

GOD'S BLESSING

On September 10, 2009, I was sitting on the couch just taking it easy when I heard a horn blow outside. It was the mail lady with a certified letter from my attorney's office. I opened it up, and it was about the third-party claim. When I read it, it said that witnesses claimed I ran a red light, hit another car, and then flipped.

I understand what the witnesses are saying, but the truck I was driving is not a fast one, even without a load. I had nine yards of cement on the truck. That extra weight would have made it even slower. I was on Winchester Road. From what I was told, there was a Family Dollar store right there at the light on the corner, and I was told my tire marks started way before the store. I really don't remember any of this, and I don't even know what made me hit the brakes. That would have been my third case with them. It's not going to go through, but I still have two cases that I know for sure are moving forward.

Sunday night, I was chilling at my mom's house having dinner. My momma, my stepdad, my sister, her husband, my nephew, and his girlfriend had all just made it back from their cruise the day before. Everybody's belly was full. My mom and I were sitting in the den watching TV. Everyone else was at the table talking, and my accident popped up in conversation. I was just laying there listening, because by me still being here through all of this, I'll probably be hearing about it for the rest of my life. I ain't mad. I'm blessed.

Friday, October 8, 2009, I talked to Mrs. Bramlett's secretary, and she told me that Mrs. Bramlett had made her determination on my vocational disability rating. She rated it at 100 percent. I'm headed back down to my mom's house. I'm staying with her and the man I've been calling Daddy for years. My mom had knee replacement surgery, so I'm staying with her until she gets better. That's Mommy—the love of my life.

Dr. Anderson is my care doctor now, and he recommends that I have more therapy set up because the stiffness in my neck was really bad. I'm back in therapy now, three days a week. I have 12 visits scheduled. Each visit is one hour, and I have two visits left until I'm done. This time, I plan to stay on top of it.

They told me that for the rest of my life, I'll need to do at least 30 to 45 minutes of therapy a day. That shouldn't be too bad. Even though they had worked with me in the past, they had only treated me based on symptoms or how I told them I felt at the moment. This time, I brought them my X-rays, and they just could not believe I was there talking to them. What I had was a human decapitation.

Well world, my case is about over. My settlement is nearly complete. I can go on living without the wonders and worries about how things will turn out. I shouldn't be worried anyway because GOD had my back, so whatever happens will be meant to happen—because it will be through Him.

As far as getting up every morning and going to work to earn a weekly paycheck—that part of my life is probably over. But yes, my Lord has sent me two blessings: He has blessed me with my life, and He has also blessed me financially. My truck-driving career may be done, but I just want to thank God it wasn't my life that ended.

God bless you, and thank you for listening.

**These are the two men God put in my life to be a part of my blessing. Chad Tillman and Andrew Smith rescued me from my overturned truck.